The World of Psychology
Readings in Diversity from

The Washington Post

Copyright © 1993 by Allyn & Bacon, a Division of Simon & Schuster, Inc.
and
The Washington Post.

10 9 8 7 6   97 96 95

Table of Contents

Intro Topics

The Washington Post

World Of Psych: Readings in Diversity

#		Biology/Brain	Consciousness	Learning	Intelligence/Cognition	Development	Motivation/Emotion	Sexuality/Gender	Health/Stress	Abnormal/Therapy	Social Psych/Appl.
1	**Brain May Determine Sexuality:** Node Seen As Key to Gay Orientation	✓						✓			
2	**Science and Sensitivity:** Primates, Politics and The Sudden Debate Over the Origins of Human Violence	✓					✓				
3	**Wide Gender Gap Found In Schools:** Girls Said to Face Bias in Tests, Textbooks and Teaching Methods			✓	✓						
4	**Shrugging Off The Burden of A Brainy Image:** Asian–American Students Say Stereotype of 'Model Minority' Achievers Is Unfair				✓	✓					
5	**Study Challenges Theory of Speech Development:** Babies Appear to Learn Phonetic Distinctions in Language Before Understanding the Meaning					✓					
6	**Race: Gray Area of Health Data:** Researchers Seek to Explain Disparities in Disease, Death Rates								✓		
7	**Between The Sexes, Confusion At Work:** Harassment Is Widespread, and Its Effects are Long–Lasting							✓			✓
8	**Gender Bias In Health Care Is No Myth:** Discrimination Against Women Occurs in Research and Treatment					✓		✓	✓		
9	**The Growing Presence Of Women In Psychiatry:** Will Sex Role Stereotypes Be Overturned?							✓		✓	
10	**At VA Hospital, 'Medicine Man' Helps Indians Try To Beat An Old Nemesis:** Rite of Purification in 'Sweat Lodges' Used in Alcoholism Treatment		✓						✓	✓	
11	**Sorting Through The Chaos Of Culture**										✓
12	**The Subtler Shades Of Racism:** Private Emotions Lag Behind Public Discourse										✓
13	**Prejudice Is In The Eye Of The Beholder, Poll Indicates**										✓

Brain May Determine Sexuality

Node Seen As Key To Gay Orientation

By Curt Suplee
Washington Post Staff Writer

ARE HOMOSEXUALS BORN GAY AND HET- EROSEXUALS BORN STRAIGHT? OR IS sexual orientation shaped by some combination of upbringing, choice and environment? That debate, which has prompted furious controversy in science and society for centuries, is likely to explode again as a result of new evidence that homosexuality may have a biological component.

Neuroscientist Simon LeVay of the Salk Institute in San Diego reports in today's issue of *Science* that, in at least one critical region, the brain structures of gay and straight men appear to be dramatically different.

The area LeVay examined, part of a deep interior formation called the hypothalamus, is known to be involved in regulating sexual behavior. One tiny node of the hypothalamus, LeVay's tissue studies found, is nearly three times larger in heterosexual males than in homosexual men.

The research also disclosed that the size of the node—which is about as big as a grain of sand and contains only a few thousand nerve cells—is remarkably similar in women and gay males.

"If this research holds up," said psychiatrist Richard C. Pillard of Boston University School of Medicine, "it would be the first physiological difference of this kind ever shown."

It is unclear whether the size of the node might have an active role in determining sexual orientation. It could also, LeVay emphasized, be an effect of sexual orientation or simply a nonsexual anatomical feature that happens to be correlated with homosexuality. But based on current understanding of brain development, he concluded, it "seems more likely" that the size of the critical cell area "is established early in life and later influences sexual behavior."

Neuroscientists long have known that certain cell clusters called interstitial nuclei on the front of the hypothalamus control sexual behavior and that those structures are much larger in men than in women.

Experiments have shown that when those nodes are damaged in male monkeys, heterosexual behavior is impaired but sexual drive remains intact. So LeVay set out to investigate whether the node would be large in "individuals sexually oriented toward women" and small in those attracted to men, no matter what their sex.

He obtained brain tissue from routine autopsies of 41 persons who died at several hospitals in New York and California. Nineteen were homosexual men who died of complications of AIDS, 16 were "presumed" heterosexual men (of whom six were intravenous drug users who also died of AIDS) and six were heterosexual women, one of whom died of AIDS.

Ironically, the conditions that made LeVay's findings possible could cast doubt on his results. Because sexual orientation is not usually noted on death records, "brain tissue from individuals known to be homosexual has only become available as a result of the AIDS epidemic," he said, and because the disease can affect the brain, "I was worried that the difference might be caused by AIDS." That is unlikely, he concluded, because the size difference was pronounced between heterosexuals who had AIDS and homosexuals who had AIDS. Nonetheless, LeVay said, to confirm his findings, "we need tissue from gay men who died of other causes."

> **One tiny node of the hypothalamus, LeVay's tissue studies found, is nearly three times larger in heterosexual males than in homosexual men.**

LeVay's work—which follows a report from Holland last year showing apparent gay/straight differences in another, non-sex-related part of the brain—is expected to reinforce the position of those who believe that sexual orientation is largely determined by heredity rather than social or environmental factors.

That is also the emerging consensus policy of the American Psychiatric Association (APA). "We do tend to feel that there probably is some kind of genetic link," said Richard Isay, a psychiatrist at Cornell Medical College and chairman of the APA's committee on gay, lesbian and bisexual issues.

As recently as 20 years ago, that was a heretical notion. Until then the medical establishment had generally regarded homosexuality as a disease. Such views, which arose as early as the late 18th century, persisted until 1973, when the APA removed homosexuality from its official roster of mental illnesses.

For most of the 20th century, the prevailing concept (still embraced today by orthodox Freudians and some other psychoanalysts) has been that male homosexuality originates in failure of the child to separate himself from feelings of "unity" with the mother in early infancy and to begin to identify with the father. Some theorized that this situation was caused by malfunctions in the "Oedipus complex," a phase in which a boy is presumed to compete with his father for the affections of his mother. Others stressed the role of withdrawn fathers or neurotically possessive, "binding" mothers in preventing development of the son's independent male identity.

In recent years, however, that classic psychoanalytic view has been challenged by two forms of research.

The first, based on extensive clinical studies of male homosexuals, indicates that there is little, if any, discernible difference between gays and straights in terms of family backgrounds and parental dynamics. "There seem to be just as many binding mothers and absent or aloof fathers among heterosexuals as among homosexuals," Isay said. "In general, we believe now that environmental factors do not play a significant role in the origins of homosexuality, although they may have an influence on the way sexual orientation is expressed."

A second line of research has turned up considerable evidence for a genetic influence on homosexuality. "We know that being gay runs in families," said Pillard, the Boston University psychiatrist, who has conducted studies of the phenomenon. Gay males, he said, appear to be about four to five times more likely to have bisexual or homosexual brothers than heterosexuals (22 percent compared to 4 percent). Studies of identical twins usually confirm those patterns.

But because there are rare instances in which identical twins adopt different sexual orientations, Pillard said, "we conclude that there must be some environmental factor playing a role, as there is in every behavior—some mixture of nature and nurture that shapes the outcome."

Further clinical evidence for a "strong genetic component," Isay said, can be seen in the very early onset of homoerotic fantasies of boys: "They seem to turn up at ages 3, 4 and 5—the same age at which heterosexual fantasies arise—and are usually directed initially toward the father just as heterosexual fantasies are directed to the mother or mother surrogate."

Moreover, if homosexuality were chiefly determined by social factors, its frequency presumably would have fluctuated considerably during the radical changes in American society since the mid-1940s, when Alfred Kinsey conducted his pioneering research into sexual behavior. Yet the reported incidence of homosexuality has remained relatively constant, Isay said. That is, "about 4 percent of adult white males are exclusively homosexual throughout their lives after adolescence, {and} about 10 percent of the total {American male population are exclusively homosexual for at least three years sometime between the ages of 16 and 65," he wrote in "Being Homosexual."

However, Isay noted, "the only way to define homosexuality is not in terms of behavior, but in terms of internal fantasy—the object of desire. Otherwise, what do you do about a heterosexual priest who is abstinent, or a gay male whose behavior is inhibited because of social pressures or internal conflict?"

Finally, if homosexual disposition derives from hereditary causes, then one might reasonably expect it to occur in other kinds of living things with whom we share genes. In fact, homosexuality "exists in virtually every animal species that has been exhaustively studied," Pillard said. There is substantial evidence for male homosexual activity in species from monkeys to manatees, and female homosexuality is not unknown. Domestic cows will mount one another when bulls are unavailable; and female-female coupling has been observed in five species of sea gulls. In fact, zoologists Gerald and Lee Durrell wrote in "Ourselves and Other Animals," it is possible that "a certain amount of same-sex prefer-

---

"If this research holds up," said psychiatrist Richard C. Pillard of Boston University School of Medicine, "it would be the first physiological difference of this kind ever shown."

---

ence is inevitable, if not necessary, in every social organization."

The idea that homosexuality is genetically innate has not prevented some clergymen and politicians from condemning homosexuality as an "unnatural" perversion that is treatable by counseling or therapy. Clinical evidence, Isay warned, shows that "efforts to change homosexuals into heterosexuals are harmful to self-esteem and to their development of a healthy capacity to love and feel loved."

Indeed, some sexual theorists hold that male homosexuality, far from being a perversion, may actually be the most unencumbered expression of "standard" male sexuality. Although gays and straights differ in the objects of their desires, the patterns of attraction are quite similar. Anthropologist Donald Symons has noted that gays, like their straight counterparts, tend to put a high value on youth and physical beauty, to focus extensively on purely genital aspects of sex and to place a high value on sexual variety, as distinct from the female emphasis on security, intimacy and stable pair-bonding. It is mainly heterosexual men whose innate sexuality must be adapted to suit typically female needs.

French social scientist Phillipe Aries speculated that "homosexuality, having by its nature nothing to do with procreation," represents "sexuality in its purest state" of cultural evolution in the post-Pill era in which "the orgasm has become an object of veneration."

LeVay's brain findings are also likely to rekindle interest in another hotly disputed theory: that male sexual orientation is determined by various ratios of prenatal levels of sex hormones, notably testosterone. Other research has indicated that these hormones influence differences in the way male and female brains develop, at least in animals.

In rats, LeVay noted, size differences in the brain area that corresponds to the human hypothalamic node are determined by levels of circulating male hormones at a critical period around the time of birth. "No definitive research has shown such an effect" in humans, Isay said.

However, in some cases, scientists have been able to observe the effects of fetal exposure to abnormally high levels of male hormones, brought on by adrenal malfunction in the fetus or drugs taken by pregnant women. Studies indicate that females who develop in those conditions tend to be somewhat "masculinized" in genital structure and to engage in more rough, aggressive play than other girls.

In addition, the growing body of research on hormones and brain development is uncovering a number of related conjectures. A news report in today's *Science* notes that researchers at McMaster University in Canada "have found lesbians to be twice as likely as heterosexual women to show left-hand preference on a variety of tasks; gay men also show such a trend." Since handedness has been linked to sex hormone levels during brain development, the article said, the McMaster group speculates that homosexuals might have "atypical brain organization," perhaps induced by "atypical sex hormone levels."

LeVay cautioned against hasty conclusions. "What I've found, he said, "doesn't tell us what we'd really like to know, which is a way to resolve the 'nature-nurture' controversy. But it does show that we can look for answers to these questions at the biological level."

❑

Science and Sensitivity

Primates, Politics And The Sudden Debate Over The Origins Of Human Violence

By Boyce Rensberger
Washington Post Staff Writer

DESCENDED FROM THE APES? DEAR ME, LET US HOPE IT IS NOT TRUE, THE WIFE of a 19th-century English bishop is said to have exclaimed upon hearing of Darwin's new theory. "But if it is true, let us hope it does not become widely known."

In the 130 years since Darwin, the relationship of human beings and the apes has become not only widely known but thoroughly accepted in science. Darwin saw the uncanny resemblance in anatomy, and molecular biologists today have confirmed it in DNA. The human genetic code is more than 98 percent identical to the chimpanzee code. Even to rhesus monkeys, we are as much as 94 percent genetically identical.

So it struck many in science as an anachronism for two members of Congress to declare, as they did on Wednesday, that the study of primates is a "preposterous basis" for trying to understand humans. With such language, Sen. Edward M. Kennedy (D-Mass.) and Rep. John D. Dingell (D-Mich.) demanded that Health and Human Services Secretary Louis W. Sullivan consider removing from office a scientific leader who had cited the similarity between human behavior and monkey behavior—Frederick K. Goodwin, psychiatrist and head of the Alcohol, Drug Abuse and Mental Health Administration. On Thursday, Goodwin bowed to the pressure and resigned.

Goodwin's offense was that just days earlier, at a meeting of a National Institute of Mental Health advisory committee, he had mentioned parallels between the violent behavior of young male rhesus monkeys and that of young male human beings. Drawing upon several decades of scientific study of the behavior of monkeys, Goodwin suggested this research might offer insight—especially into the increasing level of violence in inner cities. He want-

ed NIMH to undertake a "violence initiative" that would study the roots of human violence.

Goodwin went on to suggest that the rise of inner-city violence might be the result of a loss of "civilizing" social factors comparable to those in monkey society that usually keep the adolescent male's naturally violent behavior in check. Studies show that when young males leave the restraining social fabric of a monkey troop—as they do at a key stage in their lives—some become hyperaggressive, even murderous.

But Goodwin didn't phrase his case quite so carefully. That is the natural way of it for males, to knock each other off, he rambled. Also, he said, "maybe it isn't just the careless use of the word when people call certain areas of certain cities 'jungles.'"

To some in his audience—apparently those more attuned to the innuendo of politics than the cold eye of science—references to jungles and monkeys in connection with human behavior came across as ugly, racist code words. Rep. John Conyers (D-Mich.), a leader of the Black Caucus, called Goodwin's remarks "highly disturbing." To some within NIMH, Goodwin's remarks were the last straw. NIMH insiders say that group—which sees the human mind as shaped mainly, if not entirely, by learning and other environmental factors—lent support to the move to oust Goodwin.

Goodwin has long been associated with the other side, sometimes called biological psychiatry, which sees a biochemical, even genetic, basis for much of human behavior. While some say Goodwin often goes too far in asserting an innate basis for behavior, most in his wing think human beings are shaped by an interaction between genes and environment—nature and nurture. The combined results show up in the chemistry of

the brain, they assert, pointing to the growing value of certain drugs in the treatment of psychiatric diseases.

Still, not all in the biological wing were happy with Goodwin's remarks. "I have to say, he was undeniably careless and insensitive in the way he put it," said one scientist. "We have to be very careful in how we say this work applies to human beings. It is very easy to misunderstand."

Lost in the furor was the fact that the monkey research, which has been widely recognized within science for decades, applies to human beings across the board—to the extent that we share kinship with the monkeys. What's more, the most prominent data linking monkeys to people come from a long series of studies on criminals and other social deviants in Finland, the population of which is virtually all white.

The research offers insights that are not only fascinating but already proving useful. Some findings, for example, show there are specific biochemical derangements in the brains of certain kinds of violent people—exactly the same chemical imbalances found in violent monkeys—and that these can be

> **Goodwin suggested that the loss of structure in human society might be similarly responsible for the upsurge in urban violence.**

corrected with drugs. The same drugs work in both species.

What's more, today's research is the direct descendant of a famous series of experiments back in the 1960s that led to an established body of psychological thinking about human behavior about human behavior. Harry Harlow, experimenting on caged rhesus monkeys at University of Wisconsin, showed that babies deprived of a mother grew up to be severely warped in personality, unable to fit into monkey society—and that they were prone to random acts of violence.

Harlow's work also showed how important it was for very young monkeys to have access to stimulating environments—cages full of toys and, better yet, playmates—if they are to develop their full intellectual and emotional abilities. The monkey research quickly led a generation of well-educated parents—happy to accept the kinship between humans and monkeys—to load up their babies' cribs with all sorts of mentally stimulating toys.

treating emotionally withdrawn human children. Harlow's student and protege at Wisconsin, Stephen J. Suomi, now leads research at a rhesus colony that the National Institute of Child Health and Human Development runs in Poolesville, Md. Much of the research Goodwin cited has been done at Poolesville, where monkeys live in varying degrees of confinement from cages to large open enclosures, and at two islands where rhesus roam free—Morgan Island off the coast of South Carolina and Cayo Santiago off Puerto Rico.

"What we've learned from the animals in these essentially natural settings is that there are very definite personality differences among the young males," Suomi said, "and that these lead to differences in the amount of violent behavior they exhibit."

In the wild, rhesus monkeys live in large troops ranging from a few dozen animals to several hundred. Young males leave at puberty and live in "gangs" of other adolescent males, eventually seeking out a new troop and trying to join it. As Goodwin

again when the gang members try to join a new troop," Suomi said. "They go about it in very different ways."

Most of the surviving adventurous males enter a troop by challenging a resident adult male who ranks fairly high in the social hierarchy. Most who succeed then accept their position in the troop's social structure, soon becoming the simian equivalent of productive members of society.

Timid males take a different approach. They find a troop and simply tag along on the fringes, developing relationships with the lowest-ranking monkeys. From these humble beginnings, however, a male with good social skills—which depend not on heredity but how the animal was raised—may rise high in status by forming alliances with higher-ranking animals.

In many gangs, Suomi and others have found, there are always a few young males who never make it. These animals, 3 to 5 percent of the adolescent gang, will always lead troubled lives. Their fighting is not done to gain social standing but for what seems to be no reason at all. Unpredictably the monkey will explode in rage and rip into another animal. Such monkeys are perpetual outcasts—repeat offenders for whom there is no place in rhesus society.

Evidence for a dramatic biochemical difference among the personality types has emerged in recent years. Periodically on Morgan and Cayo Santiago, some monkeys are captured for medical exams, including spinal taps of the fluid that bathes the brain and spinal cord. In this fluid the scientists have discovered a striking chemical marker of violent behavior—low levels of a molecule that is a breakdown product of a substance called serotonin, a powerful messenger molecule that brain cells in all species use to carry certain signals. It has turned out that the more aggressive monkeys have low levels of serotonin and the least aggressive have high levels. Outcast males have the lowest levels.

The same chemical differences have also been found in humans and, again, the correlation is with violent behavior of a certain type. Work by Markku Linnoila and his colleagues at the National Institute on Alcohol and Alcohol Abuse has shown that persons who commit impulsive crimes—murder of total strangers, for example—have low serotonin. Men convicted of premeditated murder, on the other hand, have normal serotonin. Repeat arsonists—people who set fire to practically anything—have low serotonin. Men discharged

---

**Although he didn't cite these experiments
in monkey rearing, Goodwin
did suggest—at the meeting where he uttered
the inadvertent code words—that
NIMH's new "violence initiative" might look
for ways to identify human youngsters at
risk of developing violent
life styles and to help them develop
more socially successful skills.**

So close is the human-monkey kinship in behavioral terms, in fact, that the series of human developmental stages worked out by Jean Piaget, the late French child psychologist, is much the same as for rhesus monkeys—up to the age at which language becomes a major factor in children's behavior.

Work in Harlow's lab also provided evidence based on actual experiments—something virtually impossible using humans—that deprived and behaviorally impaired monkeys could be rescued by exposing them to younger, normal monkeys for as little as an hour a day. The same approach has been successfully applied in

correctly said in his ill-fated remarks, these "transitional" adolescents are often so physically violent that as many as half are killed before reaching adulthood.

Not all males run such a high risk of death. There are clear-cut personality types that lead to different fates. As juveniles, some young males stray farther from their home troop and engage in more rough-and-tumble play. When the first hormonal stirrings of adolescence arise, they eagerly strike out on their own. Other more timid males remain with the home troop until they are kicked out. Reluctantly they join a gang of other vagabond adolescent males.

"The personality difference shows up

from the military for repeated aggressiveness have low serotonin. Some psychiatrists say they can successfully treat humans with impulsive disorders with drugs that boost serotonin. What makes an individual's serotonin high or low? The research shows that genes play a role, as does environment, including taking certain illicit drugs. The amphetaminelike street drug "ecstasy," for example, destroys brain cells that manufacture serotonin. After a single dose, experimental monkeys become more disposed to violence. Alcohol can play a role too. The occasional drink increases serotonin briefly—helping create a sense of relaxation—but chronic alcohol use has the opposite effect.

"What interests many of us is that the serotonin levels of monkeys—and their personality differences—can be traced back to the animal's early beginnings," Suomi said. "It makes a big difference what kind of mothers they had and what their genetic heritage was. It's an interaction of the two—genes and environment—that shapes the animal's personality."

By deliberately manipulating the circumstances under which young rhesus monkeys grow up, Suomi has shown that environmental factors can reshape personality types begun under the influence of genes. Young monkeys born with low serotonin put into peer groups with only an artificial mother monkey that supplied milk grew up more likely to display impulsive, violent behavior. But those placed with especially nurturing mothers grew up to be more normal. Nurture had overcome nature.

Although he didn't cite these experiments in monkey rearing, Goodwin did suggest—at the meeting where he uttered the inadvertent code words—that NIMH's new "violence initiative" might look for ways to identify human youngsters at risk of developing violent life styles and to help them develop more socially successful skills. Following his resignation, Goodwin was named to head the very agency he was talking about. It remains to be seen whether those who reject biology as a factor in behavior—a significant contingent at NIMH—will allow that initiative to proceed. ❑

Wide Gender Gap Found In Schools

Girls Said To Face Bias In Tests, Textbooks And Teaching Methods

By Mary Jordan
Washington Post Staff Writer

THE MOST COMPREHENSIVE REPORT TO ASSESS THE GENDER GAP IN AMERICAN schools found widespread bias against girls in tests, textbooks and teaching practices—findings that set off an immediate controversy among educators.

"The bias that exists in how girls are taught is no longer blatant, but they experience it on a daily basis," said Sharon Schuster, president of the American Association of University Women (AAUW), which commissioned the report.

The Education Department, which last month proposed eliminating the only federal program aimed at promoting educational equity for girls, said the new report lacked perspective and hard data and maintained yesterday that gender-equity programs were no longer needed.

"You have to look at the larger context, at all the great strides women have made," said Diane S. Ravitch, assistant secretary for educational research and improvement at the Education Department. "This is a period of history in which there have been the most dramatic strides for women."

Ravitch cited statistics showing the percentage of female high school graduates enrolling in college is now larger than males and that the number of women who become lawyers, doctors and other professionals is rapidly increasing.

In 1970, 5 million college students were male and 3.5 million were female, a vastly different composition than in 1989, when 7.3 million were female and 6.5 million male. Likewise, Ravitch noted that only 8 percent of medical degrees were awarded to women in 1970, but 33 percent went to women in 1989.

"But quantity does not make quality," countered Mary Lou Leipheimer, co-chair of the National Coalition of Girls' Schools, who endorses the AAUW report, which is to be released today.

Leipheimer, who runs the Foxcroft School for girls in Middleburg, recited the other side of the statistical battleground: lagging pay for women compared with men, and underrepresentation of women in leadership roles in education. Women earn 69 cents on the dollar compared with equally educated men, according to a Labor Department analysis. And, while the overwhelming number of public elementary and high school teachers are women, more than 95 percent of the nation's school superintendents are men and 72 percent of its principals are men.

However, much of what the report "How Schools Shortchange Girls" focuses on is more difficult to quantify: little encouragement for girls to pursue math and science, few female role models in textbooks, and subtle teacher practices, such as calling on boys more often or gearing school and play activities more to the males.

The report by the Wellesley College Center for Research on Women is largely a

7

When boys called out, teachers listened. But when girls called out, they were told to "raise your hand if you want to speak."

compilation of existing studies by well-known researchers at Harvard, American and other universities and is believed to be the most thorough documentation of the gender gap in American schools.

Research by Myra and David Sadker, professors at American University, shows that boys in elementary and middle school called out answers eight times more often than girls. When boys called out, teachers listened. But when girls called out, they were told to "raise your hand if you want to speak."

Even when boys did not answer, teachers were more likely to encourage them to give an answer or an opinion than they were to encourage girls, the researchers found.

The study, noting the disparity between males and females in standardized math and science tests, said teachers often steered more boys than girls to those fields.

From 1978 to 1988, female scores on the SAT increased by 11 points while male scores increased by four points. However, males still outscored females 498 to 455.

In science, the gap is wider, and some studies indicate it might be increasing. On the 1988 SAT achievement test in physics, males averaged a 611 score out of 800, 56 points higher than females' average score of 555.

The scores are noteworthy because girls often received better grades than boys, leading some researchers to suggest bias in the tests, which often determine college admittance and scholarships.

Several studies have suggested that teachers encourage male students to work with laboratory equipment, especially in the more complex sciences. For instance, one study found that 51 percent of boys in the third grade had used a microscope, compared with 37 percent of girls. In 11th grade, an electricity meter had been used by 49 percent of males but by only 17 percent of females.

The study also shows that vocational education programs are often geared to males despite the fact that 45 percent of the work force is female. It also showed that

since the early 1970s, the participation of girls in interscholastic athletics has increased dramatically, but that boys still participate in them at twice the rate.

The report, timed to be released at the AAUW National Education Summit on Girls, is drawing the attention of many of the most influential education groups in the nation, including the head of the largest teachers union.

The report says some progress has been made since the enactment of Title IX, the landmark 1972 legislation banning sex discrimination in federally funded education programs. Yet, it says stereotypical images still appear in textbooks, the overwhelming number of authors and role models studied in class are male, and problems confronting women, including sexism, the higher rate of suicide among women, and eating disorders are often all but ignored in the curriculum.

"I think you can look at any situation and see the progress or see the way we have to go," said Susan McGee Bailey, director of the Wellesley research center. "But I think it's dangerous to say that because one-third of our medical students are now women" the struggle for gender equality is over. "There is a great deal more to be done."

❑

Shrugging Off The Burden Of A Brainy Image

Asian American Students Say Stereotype Of 'Model Minority' Achievers is Unfair

By Stephen Buckley
Washington Post Staff Writer

THE STEREOTYPE SAYS THEY'RE OVER-ACHIEVERS, GIFTED IN MATH AND SCIENCE. It says they study harder, get better grades and consistently outscore other students on standardized tests. Yet some Asian American students regard their status as America's "model minority" as both a blessing and a burden.

They say they grow weary of unreasonable expectations from peers and teachers, and harbor a sense that their accomplishments are rarely appreciated because everyone expects them to succeed.

"Everybody thinks you're smart, everybody thinks you know everything," said

Rowena Flores, 17, a junior at Howard High School in Washington. D.C., who emigrated from the Philippines in 1986. "One girl said to me, 'I wish I was from the Philippines so I could be smart.'"

Asian Americans are well represented in advanced placement classes and gifted and talented programs, and are often a strong presence in magnet schools, school officials said. In Alexandria, Virginia, for example, 30 percent of that system's Asian students are enrolled in gifted and talented programs. In Fairfax County, Virginia, the Thomas Jefferson High School for Science and Technology, which draws students from all over Northern Virginia, has a student enrollment that is 22.6 percent Asian.

But with such success have come high standards and extraordinary pressures, school officials, students and teachers say.

Alan Cheung, who last November became the first Asian American elected to Montgomery County's school board, worries especially about newer immigrants. He fears they will be pushed too hard by a school system that "automatically assumes they will do well. [Administrators and teachers] perceive that if a child is Asian, they don't need what other students need."

"The stereotypes may be positive. but they are not always for the benefit of the kids," said Lily Wong-Fillmore, a professor of linguistics at the University of California at Berkeley, who has studied how immigrant children adjust to American schools. "God was operating with a normal curve when he produced Asian kids. Some are remarkably bright. Some are not."

Stereotypes and parental pressure often lead to insecurity among Asian American young people, particularly middle-of-the-road students, Wong-Fillmore said. "It's a real hardship for kids who're ordinary Joe Wongs," she said.

Stan Cheung (no relation to Alan Cheung), a sophomore at Wilde Lake High School in Columbia, learned in grade school that his friends saw Asian students as workaholics who spent all their free time studying and never having fun.

Cheung didn't like that perception, so he worked at being socially accepted. "I didn't want people to laugh. I didn't want people to tease me," said Cheung, 16, whose family moved here from China about 20 years ago. "So I screwed around, basically."

Cheung said that teachers and classmates who know him aren't surprised by his C-average grades. But, he said, students unfamiliar with him see his marks and say. "'Hold up here for a moment.' They expect you to do really good."

Asian students said they are rarely confronted directly by fellow students or instructors who expect that all Asians will be academic success stories. Instead, pressure often comes in more indirect ways.

Jeff Wang, a sophomore at Montgomery Blair High School in Silver Spring, remembers attending a math camp last summer. "They tended to expect people like me to do well," Wang said. "They didn't say it, but you could feel it in their attitude."

When Asian Americans do well, Wang added, "people will say, 'He's just a normal

---

"It's not the environment, it's expectations. If we put higher expectations on children, they meet those expectations."

Asian.' They expect me to achieve a lot, but they don't notice it when I do."

Myung Park, a junior at Wilde Lake High, recalls earning a mark of 78 on a social studies test this year, which tied for the highest mark in the class. His teacher "asked me what happened. She asked me if I was slacking off. I wouldn't have minded if she had talked to everybody, but she didn't."

Area school officials say that teachers' attitudes toward Asian American students have changed in recent years, as systems have placed greater emphasis on sensitivity workshops and training.

"Teachers used to think Asians were all superachievers, and I think that's changing," said Carol Chen, who works with students and their parents in Montgomery's English for Speakers of Other Languages program.

Instructors acknowledge that they're aware of the stereotypes and battle — usually successfully, they say — to resist prejudgment. However, they add, they know that some teachers stumble.

Friederika Hoppes, a teacher at Montgomery Blair who sponsors the Chinese Club, said that stereotyping occurs because "when some teachers see a pattern emerge where Asian Americans are succeeding in their intellectual pursuits, they conclude that it has something to do with race."

Asian students say that some stereotypes are reinforced by their parents, who often balk when their children express a desire to pursue professions that are not related to math or science.

"I want to work with animals, but my dad wants me to go into medicine," said Cori Liv, a junior at Howard High, whose family moved here from Cambodia in 1977. "He wants me to go back to Cambodia and help the people there. That's great, but it's just not for me."

Some Asian parents say they do push their children. And Asian cultures traditionally prize education highly.

"In China, we had worse teachers and bigger classes — maybe 50, 60 students — and I was able to learn," said Annie Chien, of Potomac, a computer scientist whose son, Steve, is a 10th-grader at Blair. "It's not the environment, it's expectations. If we put higher expectations on children, they meet those expectations."

If Steve gets a B, his mother said, "He will have to explain. If he makes a B, it means he didn't work hard enough. I think he can do better." She would prefer that he go into a science-related field, although "I probably ultimately will accept whatever he becomes." But, she said, "If he decided to become a carpenter or a mechanic, I would have a hard time. I don't think he would contribute as much to society if he did those things."

Some students say they don't mind being typecast, as long as Asian Americans are seen in a positive light. "If people want to think I'm smart, let them," said Cindy Yi, a junior at Howard High. "That's fine with me."

❏

Study Challenges Theory Of Speech Development

Babies Appear To Learn Phonetic Distinctions In Language Before Understanding The Meaning

By Boyce Rensberger
Washington Post Staff Writer

LINGUISTS GENERALLY AGREE THAT BABIES ARE BORN WITH A KEEN ABILITY TO recognize all the subtle differences among all the sounds of the world's spoken languages. New research, however, has discovered that by six months of age infants have already learned which sounds are relevant to their native language, and will eventually lose the ability to distinguish sound differences that are critical in other languages.

The finding challenges the conventional theory that babies cannot learn the phonetic peculiarities of their native language until after they understand the meanings of words, a development that rarely begins before nine or ten months of age.

The finding helps explain why, for example, native speakers of Japanese usually cannot tell the difference between the English l and r sounds. Japanese has a sound midway between l and r, and native speakers hear both as if they were the same as the middle sound.

The research also sheds light on the reason people who learn a second language after puberty seldom speak it without an accent. The brain is no longer able to hear the differences between the accented version and the unaccented.

The researchers say their finding, reported in today's issue of the journal *Science*, also has implications for theories of speech perception and language development.

"We used to think babies learned the difference between lake and rake by noticing that mommy points to different things when she says those words," said Patricia K. Kuhl of the University of Washington, who led the research. "We figured the baby

thinks, 'Ah, lake and rake are two different things.' So the difference between the sounds is remembered as two different categories, two different prototypes. What our work shows is that that isn't true. Babies learn the prototype sounds before they begin to learn meaning."

A "prototype sound," Kuhl said, is the typical version of a sound to which the brain links a number of variants, any of which could be substituted without changing the word's meaning. For example, in the word "cat," there are several slightly different

French speakers, by comparison, recognize a difference between "roux" and "rue"; but most English speakers hear both vowel sounds as oo. Such phonetic differences can also derive from intonation rather than vowel or consonant sounds: In Chinese the word that native English speakers hear as "ma" can mean mother, horse, scold or hemp, depending on tonal changes that strike most Americans as quite subtle but which native Chinese speakers easily distinguish.

The new findings were based on an experiment done on six-month-old American

> New research, however, has discovered that by six months of age infants have already learned which sounds are relevant to their native language, and will eventually lose the ability to distinguish sound differences that are critical in other languages.

ways to pronounce the vowel without changing the meaning; but if the change went so far as to make it sound like "cot," a new prototype vowel would be invoked and the meaning would suddenly shift.

Kuhl said no one knows how the infant brain does it, but that it somehow classifies all spoken sounds it hears into a few groups of similar sounds that linguists call phonemes. Among the approximately 40 phonemes of English, l and r are separate and English speakers have no trouble telling them apart.

and Swedish babies in collaboration with colleagues at Stockholm University.

First the researchers taught the babies to show that they could perceive a difference between two similar spoken sounds. Each baby sat on a parent's lap while a nearby loudspeaker repeated a computer-generated variation of a spoken sound, such as the ee in the word "fee."

At first, the baby would always turn to look at the speaker. If there was no difference between two successive sounds, the curious baby saw nothing special. If there was a difference, however, a light went on in a box above the speaker, illuminating a toy bear that started beating a drum. This was the baby's reward for turning its head whenever it noticed a change in the sounds.

The babies learned quickly that if they perceived no change, there was no reason to turn their heads.

American and Swedish babies, 32 in each country, were tested to see whether they could recognize variations in pronouncing the American ee sound, which is not used in Swedish, and in the Swedish vowel y—a sound not used in English. In American English the Swedish sound can be approximated by forming the mouth to say oo but instead saying ee.

The computer synthesized 32 variants of each prototype and played them in various combinations to both groups of babies.

When American infants listened to variations on the English ee, they didn't often notice differences. American babies turned their heads in only 33 percent of the trials. But when they heard variations on the Swedish y, they spotted the differences 49 percent of the time.

The results with Swedish babies were just the opposite. The variations on the Swedish y that sound so different to American ears came across to Swedish babies only 34 percent of the time. But when Swedish babies heard variations of the English ee, they noticed the differences 44 percent of the time.

That is, each group had already learned to hear variations on prototype sounds of its own language as the same. But the infants did not have similar categories for sounds in foreign languages.

❑

Race: Gray Area Of Health Data

Researchers Seek To Explain Disparities In Disease, Death Rates

By Lynne Duke
Washington Post Staff Writer

HARRY M. ROSENBERG, THE NATION'S CHIEF STATISTICIAN ON DEATH, appeared on a television call-in show earlier this month to talk about the nation's mortality rates. He described the latest figures, those for 1989, which showed that cancer, heart disease and other maladies had once again killed blacks sooner and at higher rates than whites.

One of the viewers, a black man, called in and asked, "'Why are you always picking on us?'" Rosenberg recalled. "I thought it was a valid question."

The caller's concern highlights what Rosenberg and other medical researchers say is a pitfall in the way American mortality statistics are generated and reported year after year. The numbers tell who is dying, from what causes and at what rate, but they do not tell why.

As a result, Rosenberg and medical researchers say, there is ample room for misinterpretation, especially where race is concerned.

From an explanatory point of view, the statistics oversimplify and "there certainly is a danger" that they can mislead, said Rosenberg, who is director of mortality statistics for the National Center for Health Statistics.

If the data on the lower health status of blacks are not explained, they can leave the public with the impression that "there's something about being black that causes that to be true or something about being white," said Harold Freeman, director of surgery at Harlem Hospital and chairman of President Bush's panel on cancer.

"I think there's a tremendous amount of stigmatizing of racial groups," said Richard Cooper, an epidemiologist at Loyola University's Stritch School of Medicine and editor of the journal *Ethnicity and Disease*, who noted that theories of black genetic inferiority, although discredited, still linger in people's minds.

This year, in a move that will put federal mortality statistics in synch with what research generally has shown, the National Center for Health Statistics will add educational attainment to the age, sex, region and race variables it already uses to analyze death data. Educational attainment is correlated with high income, job stability and health care. Statisticians believe it repre-

> **Many researchers view race as a category that describes cultural distinctions more than biological ones.**

sents an accurate portrait of socioeconomic status.

When the 1989 mortality rates are reanalyzed later this year, Rosenberg's statisticians will be able to provide an annual picture of the general impact that socioeconomic factors have on the nation's death rates.

"It will be a significant development for the health statistic system of the United States and it will help us move away from explanations and descriptions of differentials by race," Rosenberg said.

"The statistical system is beginning to catch up with clinical studies," which show that in most cases it is not "race" factors but environmental ones that are causes of the

health and other data is fraught with problems, some researchers say. Although there are visible physical differences between people categorized into different racial groups, anthropologists and geneticists have generally concluded that genetic differences do not warrant grouping people into rigid biological categories.

Many researchers view race as a category that describes cultural distinctions more than biological ones.

"In medical research there is a lack of precision about the definition of race, and

leading U.S. causes of death, said Cooper. These include heart disease, cancer, stroke and chronic lung disease. Some researchers attribute purely socioeconomic factors to the cause of death while others argue for a combination of genetics and environment.

The question, said Cooper, is: "Are there genetic differences in the susceptibility to the chronic diseases which are different between populations? In other words, if everybody eats a lot and doesn't exercise, they get fat. But are American Indians, are black Americans more likely to get fat?"

Cooper argues for socioeconomic causes. "All of the common diseases are the results of exposures to risk factors," he said. Many researchers, for instance, point to stress, diet, weight and salt intake as possible factors in creating high blood pressure.

While acknowledging the interaction between environment and genetics, Clarence Grim, director of the Drew/UCLA Hypertension Research Center in Los Angeles, has conducted research that makes the case for a genetic cause of hypertension among blacks.

Some scientists have suggested that "race" is such an imperfect tool in health and medical research that it should be abandoned, except in cases where a genetic linkage is clear.

But while he believes socioeconomic factors are responsible for the incidence in most of the common deadly maladies, Charles Curry, director of cardiovascular disease at Howard University's College of Medicine, said there is probably much more about genetics to be discovered.

"Maybe there are diseases that are more common in one race than the other because of genetic factors that we just don't know about," he said.

Murray cautioned, however, that genetic classifications are of limited value.

"There is enough variation within any group that it leads to difficulties in interpreting the results of some of the research," he said. "If I make a statement, for example, about high blood pressure, that black people tend to have high blood pressure more than white people, people then take that and attribute that to everybody in the groups, rather than appreciate that this is a statistical statement."

> ## "In genetics we try to get away from talking about race in any genetic sense because there's so much overlap between groups when you look at their genetic backgrounds."

diseases that kill, said Rosenberg, who called the addition of the education variable a "breakthrough."

"When I look at the black population and the white population regardless of educational attainment, I get a 60 percent differential" in age-adjusted death rates, he said. "But when I look at black college-educated people and white college-educated people, I will get a differential of zero or a small amount ... So then I will be able to say much of what we see overall is due to differences in education level between the two population groups."

Conversely, said Rosenberg, if the differential in black-white death rates from diabetes, for instance, remains the same after education has been taken into account, "then in the classical experimental sense ... it suggests strongly that there are some biomedical factors at work."

The most recent mortality statistics show the life expectancy of whites to be 76 years, compared to 69.2 years for blacks. Rosenberg attributed much of that difference to the rate of death from homicide and AIDS among young black men. Overall, however, blacks die at greater rates than whites from heart disease (partly because of hypertension) and cancer.

The use of race in statistical analysis of

most of the definitions are really ethnic or cultural rather than racial," said Robert Murray, a pediatrician and geneticist at the Howard University College of Medicine and a fellow with the Hastings Center in New York on medical ethics. "In genetics we try to get away from talking about race in any genetic sense because there's so much overlap between groups when you look at their genetic backgrounds."

While people do share biological similarities that society describes as "racial," those similarities do not necessarily affect health.

"You have to really ask, scientifically, if the designation of race indicates genetic differences that are related to disease," said Freeman. "I think there are some instances when you can say that is true, but they are minimal."

Those instances are primarily single-gene diseases such as Tay-Sachs, found most frequently in people of Eastern European Jewish lineage. Sickle cell anemia also is a single-gene condition. But even in this special genetic category there are caveats. Sickle cell is commonly believed to affect primarily black Americans, but it is also found in people in the Mediterranean, Middle East and South Asia.

The "great debate" over race and health is focused on the chronic diseases that are the

❏

Between The Sexes, Confusion At Work

Harassment Is Widespread, And Its Effects Are Long-lasting

By Abigail Trafford
Washington Post Staff Writer

SHE WAS 15 YEARS OLD AND WORKED AFTER SCHOOL IN A DRY CLEANERS STORE. In a few months, she would take her earnings and go to college on a scholarship—then on to medical school and a distinguished career in medical science.

But in 1934, Estelle Ramey worked from 8 p.m. to 11 p.m., cleaning dresses for 39 cents an hour. Her aunt had gotten her the job. The owner was a family friend from church. Every night, he came by the store to pick up the money earned that day. He also put his hands on her shoulders, on her arms. He touched her wrists. She would inch away from him, and he kept coming closer and closer. Although he never assaulted her, she was devastated by the feelings he provoked in her.

"I would have died rather than tell my mother," said Ramey, who today is professor emeritus of Georgetown University and a distinguished endocrinologist. "I was ashamed ... For 60 years, I've carried this inside me."

Following the allegation of sexual harassment against Supreme Court nominee Clarence Thomas, unrelated stories suddenly are everywhere. Sexual harassment is one snapshot experience that binds working women together—and separates them from male colleagues.

While there is confusion over what exactly constitutes sexual harassment, there is no confusion about how it feels. The memories are vivid. So is the shame, fear and despair.

The problem is not just a legal issue in the workplace. Sexual harassment can have profound social and psychological consequences. It usually occurs when women are in their most vulnerable period—when they are young and not yet established in the workplace or in their private lives. In most cases, sexual harassment is never reported—never even talked about. The woman may not be aware of all its effects.

But sexual harassment early in a career fuels two devastating emotions: self-doubt and distrust of others.

It also aggravates the ambivalence of many women—and many men—about the role of women in the workplace. With the flood of women into the labor force since 1960—especially women with small children—the rules of acceptable social behavior between the sexes have changed. But just about every woman who drops her toddler off at day care or has a teacher

---

"I was ashamed...For 60 years, I've carried this inside me."

---

conference because a teenaged child is doing badly in science feels that twinge of guilt that maybe she doesn't belong in the working world. Maybe she should listen to those internal ghosts held over from times past that tell her she should stay at home. Even if her MBA and her mortgage tell her she can't NOT work.

Sexual harassment, whether it's a crack about her breasts from the janitor or a leer from the vice president for sales, reinforces the self-doubt with the notion that women don't really belong in the workplace.

What is stunning is how widespread various forms of sexual harassment are, ranging from unwanted fondling and lewd propositions to hitting on women for sexual favors in return for job security. A federal study found that more than 40 percent of working women had endured behavior that fits the legal definition.

Some forms are obvious. To get personal, The Post's Health Section with 10 women staffers is a microcosm of the typical harassment encountered on the job. Some of the experiences, recounted by nearly every woman, occurred 10 or 20 years ago.

One of us, early in her career, worked for a man who kept pressing her to go out with him, to sleep with him. She rebuffed him. And then he gave her a poor performance rating in her annual evaluation. She never reported it. The situation resolved itself when her supervisor went on to another job. Experts call this the "put out or get out" category.

Another, early in her career, had a co-worker, senior to her, who kept propositioning her and making sexual remarks. She told him to stop, but he continued to bother her. She found that he was doing the same thing to another female employee. They both went to their supervisor to complain. The supervisor took the co-worker aside and told him to stop bothering the two women. The overt actions stopped, but the tension increased, and one of the women moved to another department.

Another one of us, also early in her career, was in the middle of the newsroom when an editor, who had been drinking, came up to her and thrust his head between her breasts. Stunned, she pushed him away and pretended nothing had happened. A supervisor who had seen the incident later complimented her on how well she handled it; the editor received no official reprimand.

Sometimes, it's not so clear that any harassment has taken place. One of us, early in her career at another organization, caught the eye of a senior editor. He liked her work, told her she had talent and encouraged her to write a book. He also had a reputation as a womanizer, so when he repeatedly asked her out for lunch, she felt uneasy. Was he taking her to lunch because she was good or because she was pretty? Or both?

Another Post colleague remembered her first boss and how excited she had been to work on special projects with him. It was natural for him to take her to lunch. And then one day, he leaned over, took her hand, and said: "Let's have an affair." She was devastated. It was easy to say no.

What was not easy to handle were the doubts now raised in her mind. What about tive meeting ground for men and women. Is sexual harassment to one person sexual opportunity to another? In the microcosm of the Health section, two female employees met their future husbands at work.

"Sex is always there," said Babette Wise, a social worker in the department of psychiatry at Georgetown University. "Freud was right. You can't deny the sexual component when you have males and females together."

For most professional women, it is a man who holds the door to advancement, who reinforces the professional self-image. Of course, both men and women frequently depend on mentors who pick them out, train them and recommend them for assignments that will further their career. But the experience is vastly different. For instance, a

"Most people do nothing," said psychologist Louise Fitzgerald at the University of Illinois. "They basically try to deny it. They pretend it's not going on. They'll minimize the situation—it's no big deal, it was probably a joke, he doesn't mean anything by that."

Sometimes, women succumb to the "red dress" syndrome and blame themselves: If only I hadn't worn a red dress, he wouldn't have said that. Observed Fitzgerald: "These are all internally focused responses—to deny, to distance and finally to blame yourself. Women lose their self-confidence. They feel they didn't handle it right. There probably is no best way to handle it. We tell women who have been sexually harassed: 'You did exactly the right thing for you at the time.'"

Sometimes, women feel guilty because on some level they like being the object of sexual attention. Psychologists call this the "daddy's girl" syndrome. These women want to be the apple of the older man's eye. Many have been galvanized to succeed by adoring successful fathers.

"Harassers can be terrific men," said Washington psychologist Martha Gross. "A woman in her twenties feels complimented. She wants older men to find her sexually attractive. That's how insidious sexism is."

Part of the solution is not just increased sensitivity to these issues by men but the growing confidence of women as they mature in the workplace.

Estelle Ramey, for example, landed a prize job on the faculty of a large university after finishing medical school. Forty years later at a reunion, she asked her old mentor, the eminent chairman of the department, why he chose her over the hundreds of male graduates.

He told her she was the smartest in the class; she was ambitious and hard-working. "And you know," he added, "you were nice to look at."

Professor Ramey smiled at her old mentor and thanked him. But what if he had told her this at the time?

"It would have reinforced my uneasiness as the only woman in the science department," said Ramey. "At 19, 20 or 25, my self-image was so fragile, I had to be reinforced all the time."

"Sex is always there," said Babette Wise, a social worker in the department of psychiatry at Georgetown University. "Freud was right. You can't deny the sexual component when you have males and females together."

---

the bonus he gave her, the glowing evaluation? Was it because she was good or because she was pretty?

In quid pro quo cases of sexual harassment, it is usually a male superior who promises a promotion or some kind of reward in return for sexual favors. In academia, it's known as an A-for-a-lay. Or sometimes it's an Important Person who can help advance a career. One of us in the Health Section remembers the head of a federal agency who early in her career squeezed her hand and said that he could only give her a good interview if they had dinner together.

The problem is that women—particularly young women—often cannot tell what is going on. Sometimes, the offer to help a younger woman is simply that. In the real world of the workplace, communication between men and women is subtle and not always straightforward. The language of power and the language of sex often use the same words and there is room for innuendo, mixed messages, misunderstanding.

And what about romance? In recent years, the workplace has become the most effec-

male colleague remembers the first time when the city editor noticed his work, at another newspaper. The man came over to his desk, clapped him on the back, hinted about a promotion. It never would occur to him that the boss's interest was anything but a professional blessing of his talent.

This is why men "don't get it" about sexual harassment, don't seem to understand what all the fuss is about.

A bad evaluation, attempted rape, a bonus for being bedded—men understand that. But this other, this uneasy feeling some women have, this twilight zone of what's user-friendly behavior in the workplace, this shadow of fear and distrust—men generally have a hard time figuring out what the new boundaries are between the sexes. What do women NOT want?

And women don't tell them. Women usually don't let on what sexual harassment is, when it happens or why it hurts, what devastating psychic damage it can do.

The way most women deal with sexual harassment is to ignore it. Only 3 percent of the women in the federal study who experienced harassment ever reported it.

❑

Gender Bias In Health Care Is No Myth

Discrimination Against Women Occurs In Research And Treatment

By Abigail Trafford
Washington Post Staff Writer

IT'S A SOCIALLY CORRECT MYTH THAT MEN AGE BETTER THAN WOMEN—THAT THEY seem to look younger and play harder than women of the same chronological age. Certainly, George Bush at 67 with his fanatic fitness regimens in the White House looks like an advertisement for Longevity magazine. And it doesn't take the tabloids to remind women of a certain age that their male counterparts often choose younger and younger sexual partners.

But is this really Nature's Way?

To be sure, older women have more chronic medical problems than do men of the same age. But now a spate of scientific reports suggests that the aging gap between the sexes may be, well, a man-made phenomenon. Last week, two medical journals documented how women are discriminated against in health care and medical research and don't get the high-technology treatment that men receive for the same symptoms. This bias may in part explain why older women generally suffer more disability than men do—why they seem to age less gracefully.

According to two studies in the *New England Journal of Medicine*, women are less aggressively treated for heart disease than men—even though heart disease is the leading killer of both sexes. One study of 2,231 male and female heart attack patients in 112 hospitals found that although the women had more debilitating symptoms, they were less likely to undergo a key diagnostic test known as cardiac catheterization. As a result, half as many women as men underwent coronary bypass surgery to reroute blood flow to and from the heart, circumventing blocked blood vessels. This standard heart operation is known—in men, anyway—to relieve symptoms and, in certain patients, to improve life expectancy.

Another study, in the same journal, of more than 80,000 men and women treated in the hospital for heart disease in Maryland and Massachusetts, came up with similar findings.

Now, it may be that men are getting too much treatment rather than women too little. But the growing suspicion is that women with the same or worse symptoms are not taken as seriously as men by the medical profession, especially when the problem is considered a "man's disease."

This gender bias is not confined to heart disease. According to the American Medi-

---

Until women get the same degree of medical care as men, they can expect to be, as Healy put it, "second class and less than equal."

---

cal Association's Council of Ethical and Judicial Affairs, it is also found in diagnosis of lung cancer and the use of kidney dialysis and transplantation. Middle-aged women, for example, are half as likely as men to get a kidney transplant, the AMA council reported last week. Men are twice as likely as women to undergo a key diagnostic test for lung cancer.

"Being different from men meant being second-class and less than equal for most of recorded time and throughout most of the world," Bernadine Healy, the first female director of the National Institutes of Health, wrote in an editorial in the *New England*

Journal. "It may therefore be sad, but not surprising, that women have all too often been treated less than equally in ... health care."

The NIH has already launched a special program on women's health to redress some of the inequities. A glaring example of such uneven treatment is that women were not even included in the major studies of aging until 1977.

Meanwhile, myths about aging need revision. One myth is that women must be healthier than men because they live longer. But that's true only in the Alice in Wonderland world of statistics, where average women's life expectancy exceeds men's by seven years. But it's not because women are healthier; it's largely because men succumb to more violent deaths at younger ages. War, homicide, car accidents and other injuries help explain the higher death rate of young men.

The longevity gap, moreover, is closing, because of the drop in heart disease deaths in middle-aged males. As Ruth L. Kirschstein, associate director for research on Women's Health at NIH put it: "If you get men through the 35 to 60 age period without their dying of heart disease, they are [in later decades] stronger and less frail than women."

But women might be stronger if doctors treated their symptoms of heart and kidney disease with the same aggressiveness awarded to men. They might be less frail if medical science paid more attention to their particular health concerns—menopause, arthritis, breast cancer. More female George Bushes would get out on the tennis courts if doctors knew more about preventing osteoporosis, the loss of bone density that leads to hip fractures. "Then maybe women would be in better shape and the quality of their lives would be improved," said Kirschstein.

Another myth is that as women enter the workplace and take jobs once performed only by men, their supposed health advantage will be compromised. But that hasn't happened. A survey of 1,000 professional female executives across the country found that "on average this group of executives may be in better health than had been predicted as women rose to executive positions within organizations," concluded NIH researcher Judith H. LaRosa last year in the *American Journal of Public Health*.

In other words, the key to good health is not gender but status. One reason older women don't fare as well as older men is because they generally have less social and economic clout in the earlier years. Another reason, these latest reports show, is that they receive inferior medical care. Until women get the same degree of medical care as men, they can expect to be, as Healy put it, "second class and less than equal."

❑

The Growing Presence Of Women In Psychiatry

Will Sex Role Stereotypes Be Overturned?

By Robin Herman
Washington Post Staff Writer

I N 1972, PHYLISS CHESLER WROTE HER GROUNDBREAKING BOOK, "WOMEN AND Madness," accusing traditional psychotherapy of labeling women mentally ill when they did not conform to sex-role stereotypes.

Denied an aggressive, physical way of expressing anger by society, she wrote, women retreated into depression or hysteria and were called psychotic. "A predominantly female psychiatric population in America," wrote Chesler, "has been diagnosed, psychoanalyzed, researched and hospitalized by a predominantly male professional population."

Two decades later, the demographics of psychiatry have changed dramatically. The latest figures from the American Medical Association show that women now constitute 24 percent of the practicing psychiatrists in this country. Moreover, they account for 39 percent of psychiatrists under the age of 35 and more than 40 percent of the psychiatric residents in hospitals. In the near future, if trends continue, close to half the psychiatrists in the U.S. will be female.

The flood of female psychiatrists has raised questions in the field about what impact they may be making on the practice of psychiatry. More specifically, has the influx of women helped change the definition of mental illness and set new standards for treatment, be it through drugs, surgery or analysis?

So far, information remains scarce on this question. Most research on gender differences has focused on income characteristics. A scattershot of studies shows that female psychiatrists tend to see fewer patients than male psychiatrists, spend more time with them, make less money, prefer salaried positions over private practices and have a greater proportion of female patients. They are also less likely than men to pursue an academic or research career.

But no large-scale studies have examined the impact of the therapist's gender on the success of a patient's treatment.

In the past decade, psychiatry has undergone such dramatic changes because of biomedical discoveries in the brain and changes in society's attitudes toward the roles of men and women that researchers have not isolated gender as a variable in therapy. "As every good psychiatrist is supposed to function in the same way, people haven't been willing to look at that," said Carolyn B. Robinowitz, medical director at the American Psychiatric Association, who reviewed recent literature on the gender question in "The Future of Psychiatry: Psychiatrists of the Future," an article that appeared in the July issue of the *American Journal of Psychiatry*.

Robinowitz found that female psychiatrists tend to work in organized settings as opposed to private practice, work fewer hours per week than men and earn lower incomes (possibly as a result of fewer hours, she said). The percentage of women who are board-certified in psychiatry is consistently lower than the percentage of certified men. And women in academic positions are more likely to be given less prestigious assignments and be underrepresented in administrative and leadership positions.

Robinowitz hypothesizes that many of these differences can be attributed to the fact that career demands—study time for the certification exam, participation in medical societies, the responsibility of a private practice—compete with personal family considerations during a woman's peak childbearing years. For example, women may choose group practices or health maintenance organizations to be better able to balance home and office life. Working in a salaried position might allow them more leeway for extended time with patients as opposed to the pressure of a private practice where income depends on the number of patients seen.

What's more, even these slight differences in practice patterns may be disappearing as men look for flexible life-styles as well, she said.

Paul McHugh, who has been director of psychiatry at the Johns Hopkins medical school for 16 years, cites three reasons women find the field so attractive.

For one, "women in our society are enculturated to be empathic, and psychiatry depends in part in its practice for that." Second, psychiatry "is intrinsically very interesting. I'd like to think the women who go into medicine are among the most adventuresome." And third, "It's easy for them to see that they can fit their wish to be physicians with their wish to have other roles in society. They can sustain their commitment to children, family and community."

If there are any differences in how female residents and male residents approach their jobs, said McHugh, it is that women "are so devoted to their patients, I often have to bail them out, they've taken on so much." He said the female residents may be reluctant to pass cases on to other doctors for follow-up care after treating someone on the ward and instead become overwhelmed with patients.

For many female psychiatric residents at Hopkins, the reasons they chose the field have to do with the ability to make clinical diagnoses without having to rely solely on the technology that aids or defines treatment decisions in other medical specialties.

Fourth-year resident Margaret Chisolm switched from obstetrics/gynecology. "I was surprised at how little clinical judgment you could use in ob/gyn," she said. "Everything was by the numbers. If the fetal monitor showed a certain reading, a C-section was done."

Chesler applauds the increased numbers of women in psychiatry and medicine but

"The lack of a mentor is the biggest stumbling block to a career in academics for women."

sees little has changed in 20 years in the practice of psychotherapy. Women, she says, "have been carefully trained to treat other women the way blacks have been carefully trained to treat other blacks, not with compassion but at arm's length, a cruel objectivity. Sexism, like racism, is an internalized way of perceiving reality, and those who are most victimized, most colonized by these forces, will paradoxically exhibit them more than someone less victimized."

The fact that there are more female psychiatrists than ever before, she says, "is all good, but in the short run we have not changed the medical school curriculums, the graduate school curriculums, the hospital training programs. The training programs in the psychoanalytic areas are still patriarchal and male-dominated."

Studies bear out the underrepresentation of women in psychiatric leadership roles, in academics and research. "There are not a whole lot of women with families who have made it in academics," said Chisolm. "The lack of a mentor is the biggest stumbling block to a career in academics for women."

This year at Hopkins, 20 of 39 psychiatric

residents are women. The gender ratio in the residency program has been balanced for some years now. Phillip Slavney, director of psychiatric residents, discounts the rise in female residents as a factor in changing the curriculum related to the psychiatric treatment of women. The changes, he said, were made because of society's view of women.

"We added a seminar series on psychiatric problems with special relevance for women, the burden of dual careers, why might a certain diagnosis be made more often in women than men. That came out of a greater societal awareness. It had nothing to do with who the residents are but was an aspect of psychiatry that became more noticeable."

"In educating residents, we don't want to give the idea that 'you have to be one to treat one,'" he continued.

There is also concern among some mental health leaders that the influx of women may lower the prestige of psychiatry. To be sure, the decrease in the stigma of mental illness and advances in diagnosis and treatment have all led to psychiatry's greater success in dealing with a wide range of problems.

Nevertheless, Chesler see this danger. "If we are talking about helping through listening or healing through touch or healing through exercise or compassion or through the wisdom of the heart, then we are talking about 'women's work,' which is usually not paid."

❏

At VA Hospital, 'Medicine Man' Helps Indians Try To Beat An Old Nemesis

Rite Of Purification In 'Sweat Lodges' Used In Alcoholism Treatment

By Bill McAllister
Washington Post Staff Writer

AT AGE 63, CLIFFORD BONNETT, A SIOUX INDIAN AND A WORLD WAR II VETERan, had come to the large veterans hospital along the Sauk River here to undergo four weeks of treatment for a problem as old as the white man's contact with the first Native Americans: alcoholism.

But on a bright, cloudless Saturday, Bonnett was to undergo therapy unlike that available at any of the federal government's other 171 veterans hospitals.

Slipping into a tepee near the river, Bonnett wrapped himself in a white blanket and then crawled into a small tent covered by blankets and olive-colored tarpaulins.

For more than two hours, Bonnett and five other Native Americans remained in the sweltering tent, chanting songs in their native tongues, confessing to their misdeeds in English and imploring "the Great Spirit" to help them return to their traditional roots. Physically, it was not an easy ordeal for any of them.

Moments after Bonnett entered, a "spiritual adviser"—called a "medicine man" by hospital officials—used a pair of reindeer antlers to rake more glowing, red-hot rocks into a small pit in the center of the tent. Pouring water on the rocks, the medicine man transformed the darkened tent into an inferno, with temperatures soaring to more than 100 degrees.

As some of the participants gasped for breath, the medicine man and his wife began a ritual that blended elements of a religious revival with Native American lore. The participants first were urged to block out impure thoughts and imagine they were

"spiritual adviser." His wife and daughters opened the ceremony with songs in Sioux to the earth and the sun. Then, in what Renville said was a reflection of the enhanced status accorded Indian women, his wife remained in the tent during the ceremony, where she played an active role leading the participants. A reporter was allowed to enter the tent, but was warned that "anything said inside the tent stays inside the tent."

Renville seemed wary of any discussion of the theological implications of the ceremony. "This is a way of life. It is not a religion," he said.

Here at the St. Cloud Veterans Hospital, the "sweat lodge" has been incorporated into the 12 steps of the Alcoholics Anonymous program, which the hospital has used for years to help drinkers confront their problem. For the Department of Veterans Affairs, a federal agency known more for its orthodoxy than innovation, it is what officials call a bold approach to one of the biggest problems confronting Native Americans.

It is an area that congressional investigators recently described as fraught with prob-

Health Service has not, cutting red tape to get more Native Americans into their program last fall. Ignoring potential bureaucratic roadblocks in favor of action, the VA bypassed possible questions as to whether the "sweat lodge" would pass an occupational job safety inspection. They hired medicine men on the same basis and fees as the hospital's Jewish chaplain and won the support of the facility's four chaplains in the process.

"We have some catching up to do," said Gary Berg, a Lutheran minister who serves as the chief chaplain. "I feel comfortable with someone from that culture to serve their needs rather than trying to be all things to all people. ... We should have been here 20 years ago."

Native American "spiritual advisers" such as Renville typically earn about $135 for a day's work here. Others employed directly by the chaplains' service come to counsel Native Americans, much like the chaplains.

"In the use of medicine men, really we're talking more about spiritual support than medical administration," said David H. Law, the physician who oversees such programs for the VA in Washington. But Law noted that doctors are finding that "it is hard to divorce the mind and body in many cases," adding that the medicine men "may make medical therapy more acceptable" to Native Americans who are in the VA hospitals.

Although the program is new, hospital officials are excited about its prospects because they believe it can help them reach the large number of Native American veterans here in Minnesota they believe are shunning the VA out of fear it will be insensitive to their culture. "From my perspective, Indians are afraid of large institutions, especially government institutions," said Warner Wirta, a Chippewa-Cree who serves as the hospital's American Indian liaison coordinator and who has urged officials to be more sensitive to the backgrounds of Native Americans.

"There was a feeling that something was lacking," said Sally M. McCreary, chief of the hospital's nursing service and a one-eighth Cherokee who helped establish the sweat lodge program as part of the hospital's chemical dependency program. "It gives the VA a new vision on Indian awareness," agreed Joe Nayquonabe, a Chippewa and an Army veteran who works at the hospital.

VA officials in Washington say about a half-dozen veterans hospitals in the western

---

"We have some catching up to do," said Gary Berg, a Lutheran minister who serves as the chief chaplain. "I feel comfortable with someone from that culture to serve their needs rather than trying to be all things to all people.... We should have been here 20 years ago."

---

returning to their mother's womb to recall their first thoughts as a person. If that failed, "impure thoughts" were blocking their minds, the medicine man suggested.

In the land of Americas Plains Indians, this was an onikane, "a sweat lodge," a rite of purification that Native Americans long have believed can purge their past and reunite them with the earth and its goodness.

"This is to help them deal with themselves," said Cecil R. Renville Jr., a 35-year-old Sioux from South Dakota who conducted the ceremony with the help of his wife, Diane, and two of their 10 children, April and Autumn. Once in the tent, Renville would use only "natural things," a pair of reindeer antlers, a long wooden pipe covered with red cloth, and a clutch of eagle feathers.

Renville said he shuns the term "medicine man" and prefers to be known as a

lems and neglect. At a May 23 hearing before the Senate Select Committee on Indian Affairs, the Indian Health Service, the agency with primary responsibility for the well-being of Native Americans, repeatedly was criticized for failing to carry out a 69 million dollar alcohol-abuse program mandated by Congress five years ago.

Noting that death from alcoholism is four times as common among Native Americans than for Americans as a whole, Sen. John McCain (R-Ariz) said the federal government must do better. "Our nation's first citizens need our assistance and we need ... to make sure that we are not squandering the precious resources dedicated to assist them," he said.

Here at the sprawling, 561-bed red brick veterans hospital, in a program that was not mentioned during the Senate hearings, VA officials say they have done what the Indian

United States have similar programs, although none has gone as far as the St. Cloud administration.

The local program, which costs about $2,000 a year, has been cited by VA Secretary Edward J. Derwinski as an example of how his department is working among Vietnam veterans to ease problems of post-traumatic stress disorder as well as alcoholism. "I don't think we can claim any huge success, but for some patients this is a therapeutic modality that is right," said McCreary.

The hospital adapted the program from an alcohol treatment program on a nearby reservation. Instead of attempting to transport its Indian patients to the reservation, the VA decided it would be easier to build a sweat lodge on the hospital grounds and bring a practitioner here. Patients are screened by physicians before they are allowed to enter the sweat lodge and members of hospital staff stay near the tent throughout the ceremony.

"I want to get back to my culture and my traditions," said Bonnett after he emerged dripping wet from "a very good sweat." Bonnett said he found the experience so satisfying that he was now making his goal to participate later this summer in a more arduous four-day "Sun Dance" ceremony in South Dakota.

After the ceremony ended and the Renvilles climbed into their rusting station wagon for the return trip to South Dakota, a VA official confided that they had encountered a new, unexpected problem.

Renville had decided that he could no longer accept a government check for his work; that he preferred to be paid in cash. That, the VA officials said, was likely to be a problem they couldn't quickly resolve.

❏

Sorting Through The Chaos Of Culture

By James T. Yenckel
Washington Post Staff Writer

*O*N A SALES TRIP TO JAPAN A FEW YEARS BACK, KEVIN CHAMBERS WAS INTRO-duced to a group of local businessmen, "and then I immediately launched into my sales pitch." To his surprise, they turned completely cold. They looked at the ceiling, and they wouldn't talk to me. It was very embarrassing. I tried to fill the gap with babbling, and then I just left. I couldn't imagine what in the world I had done wrong.

His mistake, as he later learned, was to assume that Japanese business meetings progress at the same fast, let's-get-to-the-point pace of American negotiations.

"I had failed to comprehend the importance of cultural differences," says Chambers. Japanese meetings typically begin with a lot of "chitchatting. They want to get to know the individual people they are dealing with, to know their character."

Americans today travel to all corners of the world, and even those with only slight cultural sensitivity have become aware that folks in other countries don't always do things the way we do at home. Business travelers fail to heed cultural differences at the peril of lost sales or contracts. Leisure travelers who ignore them may wonder why they are sometimes treated with indifference or what they perceive as rudeness.

In Asia, for example, the most ordinary gestures can lead to misunderstandings. In the United States, it is not unusual for an adult to pat the head of a small child who has been introduced by his or her parents. In Malaysia, and other Asian countries, touching anyone's head —but especially a child's—is improper and considered an indignity because the head is regarded as the home of the soul.

But even trying to be culturally aware can have its dangers. Roger E. Axtell, now a retired American businessman who has traveled extensively in the Far East, was asked to prepare a dinner toast in China. Doing the right thing, he arranged to have the toast written out phonetically in the local language, which he does not know. When it came time to speak, he thought he was saying, "Thank you very much for dinner. I've eaten so much I have to loosen my belt." But as he mispronounced the unfamiliar words, what his hosts actually heard was something to the effect that "the girth of my donkey's saddle is loose." It was, says Axtell, an embarrassing moment.

How does a traveler avoid these wholly unintentional cultural mishaps? For one thing, before you go, "do your homework," say Chambers and Axtell, both of whom have written helpful guides to familiarizing yourself with differing manners and practices abroad. Much of the content is based on their personal experiences.

> When it came time to speak, he thought he was saying, "Thank you very much for dinner. I've eaten so much I have to loosen my belt." But as he mispronounced the unfamiliar words, what his hosts actually heard was something to the effect that "the girth of my donkey's saddle is loose."

> "They do shake hands in Japan, but it's because they know we do it. We think a bow is subservience, but to them it's a sign of respect."

Chambers, who is now manager of the Asia/Pacific office of the Oklahoma Department of Commerce, is the author of *The Travelers' Guide to Asian Customs & Manners* (Meadowbrook, $7.95). Axtell, formerly the vice president of worldwide marketing for the Parker Pen Co., has just completed *Gestures, the Do's and Taboos of Body Language Around the World* (Wiley, $9.95). Each is an eye-opener into the pitfalls awaiting an unaware traveler.

Nowadays, Axtell bounces about the world on the speaker's circuit. Much of what he has to say about do's and taboos is on the lighter side, but his audiences are mainly business groups, and they also are looking for advice that will smooth their way in the international world of commerce. In his talks, as in his new book, he makes quite clear, for example, that the ordinary American handshake is not a universally accepted gesture of greeting.

In Japan, the traditional greeting among friends and business acquaintances is a polite bow, Axtell says, and Americans who observe this custom are much appreciated. "They do shake hands in Japan, but it's because they know we do it. We think a bow is subservience, but to them it's a sign of respect." In a business situation, the person on the lowest rung of the corporate ladder bows first and deepest.

The exchange of business cards in Japan is also far more ceremonial than we are accustomed to in this country. When accepting a card from a Japanese, you should examine it carefully, says Axtell, and place it in front of you rather than quickly tucking it in your coat pocket. In Japan, the card represents "one's personal identity, one's label, shingle, sign, rank and name tag—all in one." When presenting your card, do so with both hands, facing the lettering toward the recipient, and make a slight bow.

Gift-giving in Japan is quite common, and in this too there is ritual. The basic rule, says Axtell, is to make a thoughtful gift rather than a lavish one—"Substance is not as important as style." Be sure the gift is wrapped, but not in white paper—the color white symbolizes death—and do not use bright-colored paper or fancy bows. Neither is acceptable, although Axtell admits he hasn't yet discovered why.

Much of Axtell's new book, and an earlier one, *Do's and Taboos Around the World* (Wiley), focuses on advice for business travelers. But vacationers can make use of many of the suggestions. In Indonesia, for example, eating while walking on the street is deemed inappropriate, and you might cause offense if you talk to someone without removing your sunglasses. Don't take umbrage yourself, however, if a street vendor touches you to get your attention. It's the custom.

In India, the traditional greeting is palms pressed together chest high as if in prayer, a gesture accompanied with a slight bow. If you use it, says Axtell, "such a show of knowledge about Indian customs will be appreciated." If you should encounter bureaucratic indifference to a travel problem, always a possibility, don't blow your stack. "Showing anger is usually the worst way to accomplish almost anything."

In Hong Kong, to signal a waiter for the check, make a writing motion with both hands. To beckon someone else, however, you should extend your arm, palm downward, and make a scratching motion with the fingers, Axtell advises. Never, never use the index finger, palm up and curled

in Taiwan and South Korea teaching English and learning Korean and Chinese. Before his Oklahoma state job, he managed the Asia/Pacific office for a cable TV network. "That's where I made all my mistakes," he says.

As he traveled, he kept notebooks of his encounters, including that terrible first sales pitch to the Japanese. "I was always interested in why people did things differently," he says. Ultimately, he acquired the cultural savvy he had lacked and returned to get his contract. His notebooks became the basis of his guide, for which he spent a year and a half of intensive research, interviewing local people and Americans living and working in Asia. It appeared in 1988, and it has been updated in later printings.

"Lots of things have changed since it first came out," he says. "I don't call it Westernization; rather, it's internationalization"—a blending of cultures—"which is more common among the younger generations."

Still, Americans continue to blunder culturally. "I see plenty of that, he says."

"Most Americans make the mistake of being too familiar, too informal, too loud and too demonstrative," he says. "In most Asian countries that doesn't go over well. You should be more reserved, more conservative in dress. Especially in business, you have to hold back a little bit."

In many countries, the local people are not easy to get to know. Based on his travels, Chambers finds that the Thais, the South Koreans and the Taiwanese "easiest to become friends with. They are more outgoing. It's not uncommon to be approached in the street and asked where you

> "Lots of things have changed since it first came out," he says. "I don't call it Westernization; rather, it's internationalization"—a blending of cultures—"which is more common among the younger generations."

beckoningly toward you. "That gesture is used only for animals." Axtell's books are worldwide in scope; Chambers's guide features Australia, New Zealand and 14 Asian nations, and it is much more detailed—though maybe not quite so much fun to read. Chambers spent a year and a half each

are from. It never happens in Japan." Chambers's guide covers such intercultural aspects as greetings, proper conversational topics, good manners, body language, dress, tipping, table manners and business etiquette. If you must criticize someone in Hong Kong, he writes, do so tactfully and in private. "Hurting someone's feelings is a breach of courtesy." If you are the recipient of a compliment, deny it politely. "The Chinese appreciate compliments and offer them often, but consider it impolite to say 'thank you' in response."

In the Philippines, it is socially safe to talk about professions, families, children and the local culture and cuisine, he says. But unless you're gossiping with close friends, stay away from matters dealing with the country's political strife, and don't make jokes about the Ferdinand Marcos administration.

In South Korea, do not address anyone by his or her given name. "It's impolite and will make people wince visibly."

In Thailand, the feet are considered an ill-favored part of the body. Don't use them to point at anyone or to help move a heavy object, says Chambers. And don't point with your hand, especially with a single finger. It is more acceptable to use your chin.

If other people are sitting on the floor, keep off the chair. You should "never sit with your head higher than that of an older or more senior person."

Indonesians consider Westerners "too quick to anger, too serious about themselves and too committed to the idea that time is money," says Chambers. "As you conduct business, don't fret over any lost time."

There seem so many ways in which a traveler in all innocence can go wrong. But by practicing three important virtues—patience, perseverance and politeness—and by doing a bit of homework, you may be able to avoid making the most insulting gestures and end up only amusing your foreign acquaintances, says Axtell. "I'm

---

> "The Chinese appreciate compliments and offer them often, but consider it impolite to say 'thank you' in response."

---

sure I've done things people are still laughing at."

If all else fails, a smile is welcome anywhere. "As you travel around the world," he says, a smile "may help you slip out of the prickliest of difficult situations."

Axtell has written two other cultural guides, *The Do's & Taboos of International Trade: A Small Business Primer* and *Do's and Taboos of Hosting International Visitors*, both also published by John Wiley &

Sons. Axtell also recommends the following books and other publications on foreign customs and manners:

"Culturgrams", a series of 102 four-page newsletters about individual countries and their customs and courtesies. Updated annually, the set is $40; individual countries, $1. Publication Services, David M. Kennedy Center for International Studies, 280 HRCB, Brigham Young University, Provo, Utah 84602, 801—378-6528.

Japanese Etiquette and Ethics in Business and *Chinese Etiquette and Ethics in Business*, by Boye DeMente (National Textbook Co.).

The Economist Business Traveller's Guides to Southeast Asia, China, Japan and several European nations (Prentice Hall).

Getting Your Yen's Worth: How to Negotiate With the Japanese, by Robert T. Moran (Gulf).

The Travelers' Guide to European Customs & Manners, by Nancy L. Braganti and Elizabeth Devine (Meadowbrook).

Another source of cultural information is the Intercultural Press, which publishes books on cross-cultural topics. For a catalogue: 16 U.S. Route 1, P.O. Box 700, Yarmouth, Maine 04096, 207-846-5168.

❏

The Subtler Shades Of Racism

Private Emotions Lag Behind Public Discourse

By Malcolm Gladwell
Washington Post Staff Writer

*T*HE PEOPLE IN THE EXPERIMENT WERE WELL-INTENTIONED WHITE LIBERALS, MEN and women who swore they would never deliberately discriminate against anyone on the basis of race.

But then the telephone call came—a "wrong number" that turned into a request for help. The caller said his car had broken down, he had just used his last dime, and he needed someone to call a tow truck.

Whenever the psychologists in this now-classic study had an identifiably black voice make the call, the participants were six times more likely to hang up prematurely than when the call came from someone who sounded white.

"I thought that liberals weren't going to discriminate. I thought they were going to

21

be the great white hope," said Samuel Gaertner, the University of Delaware psychologist who conducted the study. "But it didn't work out that way. In a number of situations we found that well-intentioned people do in fact discriminate."

Gaertner's study was one of the first to describe the phenomenon known within psychological circles as aversive racism. This is not the open and deliberate prejudice of the Ku Klux Klan. Nor does this term refer to people who are racist but who lie about it.

Rather, psychologists describe this as more subtle. These are the subconscious, discriminatory acts and feelings of people who genuinely do not want to be that way. This is the racism of people who would vote for a black president but might unconsciously steer away from sitting next to a black person on the Metro.

Aversion and Persistent Discrimination
In the more than 10 years since the Gaertner experiments, dozens of field and laboratory

---

Aversive racism differs from more virulent forms in several ways. One is a matter of degree. It is rarely expressed in terms of overt hate or hostility, but surfaces instead in less dramatic feelings of discomfort, uneasiness, disgust or fear.

---

experiments have explored aversive racism, which is now considered by many psychologists to be the most common form of racism in the United States. The theory of aversive racism is used to explain why discrimination persists in a country where more than 85 percent of whites routinely profess in opinion polls to hold exemplary attitudes on race relations.

But even after years of study, aversive racism remains something of a mystery. Researchers don't know whether blacks have the same kind of feelings toward whites. Nor do they know to what extent this kind of modern racism is conscious.

Did the self-described liberals on the phone, for example, hang up quickly on the black voice without realizing they had made a racially discriminatory judgment? If so, the prospects for improvement seem dim. Or were they aware of their feelings but, as

with a bad habit, unable to stop the reflex? If this is the case, psychologists see some hope for changing attitudes.

"There are two ways of looking at it," said John Dovidio, a Colgate University psychologist who, with Gaertner, has been among the leaders in psychological research into prejudice. "You can see this as a new form of racism which is a necessary step toward its elimination—people who haven't yet been able to overcome their natural biases. ...The other possibility is that this could be the mutant of the virus that is resistant to change. We used to get rid of racism by saying it was bad, illegal or immoral. But with modern racism, that message doesn't produce any real change in behavior because people don't think it applies to them."

Aversive racism differs from more virulent forms in several ways. One is a matter of degree. It is rarely expressed in terms of overt hate or hostility, but surfaces instead in less dramatic feelings of discomfort, uneasiness, disgust or fear. It is also not a consistent response, but slips out inadvertently in situations when the rules of socially correct behavior are ambiguous.

In one experiment by Gaertner and Dovidio, for example, subjects who professed not to be racist were told they were going to participate in an ESP experiment with another person in an adjoining room, who was actually a confederate in the experiment. The subjects were introduced to the person before the experiment and could see whether they were black or white. After the putative ESP experiment started, the subject would hear the sound of chairs falling and the confederate calling out for help. The researchers counted how often the subjects came running.

What they found was that the race of the person in distress made a difference only under certain circumstances. If the subjects thought they were the only ones who could

hear the "accident," they almost always responded. But if the subjects were told there were several other people listening to the confederate, they were only half as likely to respond to blacks in distress as to whites in distress.

In other words, when their social responsibility to help was unambiguous, the subjects didn't discriminate. But when it wasn't so clear, when it was possible to rationalize inaction, the buried prejudices surfaced.

The same two researchers also did an experiment in which whites who professed to have liberal attitudes on race were introduced to a confederate who was supposed to help them in carrying out a fairly complicated task. The confederate was identified either as their supervisor or their subordinate and described privately as being either of high ability or low ability. After the introduction, the confederate "accidentally" knocked over a can of pencils.

The experimenters found that the subjects were more likely to come to the aid of blacks described as being of low ability than to help low-ability whites. They also were far more likely to be helpful to blacks introduced as their subordinates than to supervisory blacks. When the other person was white, the subjects had the opposite reaction—they helped white supervisors but not white subordinates.

Debate Over Awareness of Prejudice
Once again, in other words, the underlying racism of those who professed racial tolerance was not simple, crude bigotry. They didn't mind helping blacks in a jam. But they were most likely to help those blacks who fit the racist stereotype of being of low status and intelligence.

Psychologists say these buried prejudices, which their studies show to be endemic among white Americans, are holdovers from an earlier, more racist era. While American public discourse has largely been cleansed of racism, they say, private emotions have lagged behind, repressed by people who no longer find them personally or socially acceptable.

"The majority of people who say they are not prejudiced probably are at some level," said Dovidio. "Most whites don't have the necessary experience and cultural background to make them truly non-racist."

But how deeply have these emotions been buried? Dovidio and Gaertner interpret their studies to mean that aversive racism is completely below the level of awareness, that those who practice it have no inkling of what they are feeling, saying or doing.

Others disagree. In a number of recent papers, University of Wisconsin psychologist Patricia Devine argues that liberals are aware of those instances in which their personal convictions are contradicted by their actions and actually feel guilty about it.

She said this makes her optimistic. Because people are aware—if only belatedly—of their prejudice, she believes they can act on it, and their guilt can serve as a motivator.

"I look on reducing prejudice as the breaking of a bad habit, she says. It's like biting your nails or weight regulation.

People have a goal they are trying to achieve and sometimes they succeed and sometimes they fail. But ultimately they will learn how to internalize their feelings and learn how to conquer it."

❑

Prejudice Is In The Eye Of The Beholder, Poll Indicates

By Richard Morin & Lynn Duke
Washington Post Staff Writers

WHITE PREJUDICE AGAINST BLACKS IS WIDESPREAD, BOTH WHITES AND BLACKS agree, but they differ sharply on whether racism remains a major impediment to black advancement, a new Washington Post national survey shows.

Nearly half of the whites questioned in the poll agreed that "most whites have prejudiced views about blacks," a view expressed by more than six of ten blacks.

Only about a third of the whites saw racism as an impediment to black advancement. But seven of ten blacks agreed with the statement.

This profound difference in black and white views on the effect of white racism reflects what Lawrence Bobo, a UCLA sociologist and authority in racial attitudes, calls "laissez-faire" racism.

"A fair number of whites do acknowledge that discrimination exists, in the labor market, in the housing market, in other domains," Bobo said. Still, whites believe "that the core problem is that blacks aren't working hard enough, or aren't sufficiently motivated … 'It's [blacks'] fault, it's what the free market produced, it's what they chose to be.'"

This disparity in black and white views on the effects of racism was apparent in a series of focus groups conducted for *The Washington Post*. Bobo and Marylee Taylor, a social psychologist at Pennsylvania State University and another researcher in racial attitudes, were invited to observe. Bobo is black, Taylor is white.

In the groups, whites acknowledged that discrimination continues, but they suggested that blacks were holding themselves back by not fully embracing the values of hard work and personal responsibility. The blacks, who said they do in fact embrace those values, suggested that subtle forms of racism and outright white advantage remained barriers to blacks.

The diverging views reflect the different exposure that each group has to the race

the majority of whites in the survey, saying past discrimination did not justify giving blacks government help that whites do not receive.

"They see and experience efforts to move blacks into the positions they hadn't had in the past," Bobo said. And although the whites in the group had not personally lost an opportunity to a black, Bobo said their fears appeared to be based on the correct belief that "the category I belong to, the group I'm in, doesn't have the same access we used to."

But Bobo said, "There seems to be a fair

Only about a third of the whites saw racism as an impediment to black advancement. But seven of ten blacks agreed with the statement.

---

issue, Taylor said. "Black people are much more likely to be aware of race for more of their waking hours than whites are." Blacks generally have more clearly formed ideas about race than whites, she said.

"This means that white Americans are capable of a wide range of responses when racial questions do come their way," she said. "And they are not necessarily consistent."

Whites in the focus groups agreed with

amount of exaggeration that goes into it. There seems to be, at least in the discussions we heard in the groups, a real preparedness, an eagerness, to believe the worst-case scenario." This suggests to him that fears of reverse discrimination go beyond purely cost-benefit thinking to something that has an emotional element to it that might even be called prejudice."

For instance: focus group participants

> ## "Black people are much more likely to be aware of race for more of their waking hours than whites are."

were presented with a hypothetical hiring scenario in which they had to decide which of two equally qualified candidates they would hire, one black and the other white. Some of the whites in the group said they would feel most comfortable with the white candidate.

"They didn't seem by and large to make the connection between acting on their level of comfort and how that generalizes to a pattern of black disadvantage, where if this situation happens in repeated cases you get the gradual closing out of blacks," Bobo said.

Some blacks in the scenario also opted for the job candidate who was black. But Bobo said the black and white choices are quite different.

"At one level it does seem to be parallel, that both groups in a somewhat ethnocentric manner are saying they're going to do what's most comfortable," he said. But he added, "There's social asymmetry there" because it is black disadvantage, not white disadvantage, that is a continuing social problem.

For the blacks in the focus groups, there was deep frustration. On one hand, the blacks were concerned about the persistence of prejudice. At the same time, they were concerned that blacks were not doing more to solve the economic and social problems in their communities.

This latter concern was reflected in the national survey, in which about half of the blacks said blacks could do just as well as whites if they would only try harder.

For both whites and blacks, talking about race is difficult. Half of the whites and two of three blacks in the Post poll agreed with the statement "it is hard for white and blacks to talk honestly about race relations."

In the focus groups, however, the talk was candid and several of the participants later reported new racial insight they had gained through the discussion. This outcome, Bobo and Taylor agreed, suggests that frank talk and contact between the groups can lead to greater racial understanding and an easing of tensions. "A vision of the possible," Bobo said.

❏